Real Estate Economics
Property Market Principles and Practices

By Willem Tait

Published by WRT Publishing

Copyright © 2024 by Willem Tait
All rights reserved.

Copyright Warning:

No part of this publication may be reproduced, distributed, or transmitted in any form or by any means, including photocopying, recording, or other electronic or mechanical methods, without the prior written permission of the author, except in the case of brief quotations embodied in reviews and certain other noncommercial uses permitted by copyright law.

For permission requests, contact the author at:
willemtait@outlook.com

Disclaimer:

This eBook is for educational and informational purposes only. The author is not liable for any damages or losses arising from the use or misuse of the content in this book.

Cover Design: Time Brands
Published by WRT Publishing
First Edition

Library ISBN Print 978-0-6398577-2-5
Library ISBN eBook 978-0-6398577-3-2
Amazon KDP ISBN Paperback 9798304610780
Amazon KDP ISBN Hardcover 9798304617871

Why this Book?

If you have ever wondered why property prices rise, why some markets boom while others crash, or what really drives the value of land and buildings, this book gives you the answers.

Real Estate Economics takes you inside the engine room of the property world, breaking down the hidden forces that shape every market. It is written for anyone who wants to think smarter about real estate, whether you are buying your first home, investing for growth, or simply curious about how cities and economies evolve.

You will not find empty jargon or complicated charts here. Instead, you will find clear explanations, practical insights, and real-world logic that help you see opportunities others miss.

Keep reading, because once you understand how real estate economics works, you will never look at property the same way again.

Introduction

Real estate isn't just about buying and selling properties; it's about understanding the forces that shape the world we live in.

Behind every towering skyscraper, bustling neighborhood, or quiet suburban street lies a story, a dynamic interplay of economics, planning, and human ambition. *Real Estate Economics* unravels these stories, peeling back the layers of complexity to reveal the principles that govern one of the most exciting and impactful industries in the world.

This book is your gateway to understanding how real estate markets work, why prices rise and fall, and how global trends ripple through local neighborhoods. It's a journey into the heart of real estate, where supply meets demand, policies shape cities, and innovation redefines what's possible.

Whether you're a first-time investor, an experienced developer, or simply someone curious about how cities grow and evolve, this book is for you.

But here's the thing: *Real Estate Economics* isn't just another book filled with dry facts and figures. It's a conversation, one designed to make you think, to spark your curiosity, and to equip you with the knowledge to see opportunities where others see complexity.

From understanding the basics of market dynamics to exploring the future of smart cities and sustainable development, this book connects the dots in ways that are practical, insightful, and deeply engaging.

And it doesn't stop at understanding. This book is a call to action, a roadmap for applying what you learn to real-world scenarios.

Whether it's navigating market cycles, evaluating property values, or spotting trends before they happen, *Real Estate Economics* empowers you to act with confidence and foresight.

By the time you reach the final chapter, you'll not only have a solid grasp of the principles shaping real estate but also the tools to shape your own journey, whether it's building an investment portfolio, planning a development, or simply appreciating the incredible complexity of the markets that touch all our lives.

So, why read this book? Because real estate isn't just about properties; it's about possibilities. Every chapter is an opportunity to see the world differently, to understand the forces that connect economies, cities, and people.

And here's my promise: with every page, you'll feel closer to the heart of real estate economics, armed with knowledge and inspired by ideas.

You've already taken the first step by opening this book. Now, turn the page, and let's embark on this journey together.

There's so much to discover, and it all starts here.

Table of Contents

Why this Book? 1
Introduction 3
Table of Contents 6
Chapter 1: Introduction to Real Estate Economics . 16
    What Is Real Estate Economics? 18
    Real Estate and Economics 20
        For Individuals: 20
        For Societies: 20
    Five Key Real Estate Economic Concepts 22
        1. Supply and Demand 22
        2. Market Cycles 22
        3. Location 23
        4. Government Policies 23
        5. Interest Rates 23
    Why Real Estate Economics Matter 24
    Preparing for the Journey Ahead 25
Chapter 2: Economic Indicators and Real Estate Markets 26
    What Are Economic Indicators? 28
    Key Economic Indicators and Their Impact on Real Estate 29
        1. Gross Domestic Product (GDP) 29
        2. Inflation 29
        3. Employment Rates 30

    4. Interest Rates 31
    5. Housing Starts and Building Permits 31
Interpreting Economic Indicators 32
A Real-World Application: Economic Indicators in Action 33
The Importance of Staying Informed 34
Conclusion: Reading the Signs 35

Chapter 3: Supply and Demand Dynamics 36
The Fundamentals of Supply and Demand in Real Estate 38
Factors Influencing Supply 39
    1. Land Availability 39
    2. Construction Costs 40
    3. Government Policies and Regulations 40
    4. Market Cycles 40
Factors Influencing Demand 41
    1. Population Growth 41
    2. Income Levels and Employment 41
    3. Interest Rates 42
    4. Consumer Confidence 42
The Interplay Between Supply and Demand 43
    1. Supply Shortages and Price Increases ... 43
    2. Oversupply and Price Drops 43
    3. Elasticity in Real Estate Markets 44
Real Estate Sectoral Dynamics 45
    Residential Real Estate 45
    Commercial Real Estate 45
    Industrial Real Estate 46
Practical Applications: Using Supply and

Demand to Your Advantage 47
A Real-World Case Study: The California Housing Crisis..48
Conclusion: The Balancing Act........................49
Chapter 4: Market Cycles and Trends 50
The Nature of Market Cycles 51
    1. Expansion 51
    2. Peak...51
    3. Contraction..52
    4. Trough..52
Factors Driving Market Cycles 53
    1. Economic Conditions 53
    2. Consumer Behavior 53
    3. Government Policies..............................54
    4. Global Events..54
Identifying the Four Real Estate Market Trends 55
    1. Demographic Trends 55
    2. Technological Advancements 55
    3. Sustainability and Green Building 56
    4. Urbanization and Suburbanization..........56
Predicting Three Market Cycles and Trends 57
    1. Analyzing Historical Data 57
    2. Monitoring Leading Indicators.................57
    3. Staying Informed.....................................57
Practical Applications: Navigating Market Cycles 58
Real-World Case Study: The 2008 Financial Crisis 59

Conclusion: Timing Is Everything 60
Chapter 5: The Impact of Interest Rates..................61
What Are Interest Rates? 62
The Connection Between Interest Rates and Real Estate 63
    1. Property Values 63
    2. Mortgage Affordability 64
    3. Investment Decisions..........................64
The Broader Economic Impact 66
    1. Consumer Spending 66
    2. Construction Activity 66
    3. Employment Trends............................67
Historical Examples of Interest Rate Impacts...68
    The Early 2000s Housing Boom 68
    The COVID-19 Pandemic 68
Predicting Interest Rate Trends 69
    1. Central Bank Policies...........................69
    2. Global Economic Conditions..................69
    3. Market Sentiment................................69
Practical Applications: Navigating Interest Rate Impacts 70
A Real-World Case Study: The UK Housing Market..71
Conclusion: The Power of Percentages 72
Chapter 6: Government Policies and Regulations ..73
The Role of Government 75
    1. Regulators..75
    2. Participants 75
Key Areas of Government Impact....................76

- 1. Zoning and Land Use Regulations..........76
- 2. Tax Policies...77
- 3. Affordable Housing Initiatives 77
- 4. Infrastructure Development.....................78
- 5. Environmental Regulations 79
- How Policy Changes Affect Real Estate...........80
  - 1. Economic Stimulus Measures.................80
  - 2. Regulatory Tightening............................81
  - 3. Political Changes 81
- Historical Examples of Policy Impact on Real Estate..82
  - 1. Singapore's Cooling Measures 82
  - 2. The U.S. New Deal 82
- Practical Applications: Navigating Government Policies 83
- Conclusion: The Policy Puzzle 84

Chapter 7: Real Estate Valuation Methods 85
- Why Real Estate Valuation Matters 86
- Key Real Estate Valuation Methods 87
  - 1. Sales Comparison Approach (Market Approach) 87
  - 2. Income Approach...................................88
  - 3. Cost Approach 89
  - 4. Automated Valuation Models (AVMs).....90
- Four Factors Influencing Valuation 91
  - 1. Location 91
  - 2. Market Conditions 91
  - 3. Property Characteristics.........................91
  - 4. Economic Indicators...............................92

Applying Valuation Methods to Different Property Types 93
    Residential Properties................93
    Commercial Properties 93
    Unique or Special Properties 93
The Role of Valuation in Urban Economics and Global Markets................94
    Urban Economics and Development 94
    Global Real Estate Markets 95
Practical Tips for Applying Valuation Methods .96
    For Buyers and Sellers 96
    For Investors 96
    For Developers 96
Conclusion: Unlocking the Value Puzzle 97

Chapter 8: Urban Economics and Development 98
What Is Urban Real Estate Economics?................100
The Role of Urban Planning in Real Estate Development................101
    1. Land Use and Zoning................101
    2. Infrastructure Development................102
    3. Sustainability and Smart Cities 102
Urbanization and Its Impact on Real Estate ...104
    1. Population Growth and Housing Demand 104
    2. Economic Clusters and Real Estate 104
    3. Gentrification and Urban Renewal 105
Challenges in Urban Development 106
    1. Affordable Housing 106
    2. Traffic Congestion................106

    3. Environmental Concerns........................106
  Case Studies: Urban Economics in Action 107
    1. London's Crossrail Project.....................107
    2. The Transformation of Detroit...............107
  The Role of Valuation in Urban Development 108
  Practical Applications: Navigating Urban Economics 109
  Conclusion: Cities as Engines of Growth........110

Chapter 9: Global Real Estate Markets...................111
  What Makes International Real Estate Unique? 112
    1. Diverse Market Dynamics 112
    2. Currency Fluctuations 113
    3. Cultural Preferences 113
  Drivers of Global Real Estate Markets............114
    1. Economic Growth and Urbanization 114
    2. Cross-Border Investments 114
    3. Technology and Connectivity................115
    4. Geopolitical Factors 115
  Asset-Backed Mortgages in International Markets 116
    What Are Asset-Backed Mortgages?........116
    Benefits of Asset-Backed Mortgages........116
    Challenges of Asset-Backed Mortgages...117
  Strategies for Navigating Global Real Estate Markets 118
    1. Research Local Markets 118
    2. Diversify Investments............................118
    3. Leverage Professional Networks 119

4. Monitor Global Trends 119
Case Studies: Global Real Estate Dynamics .. 120
   1. Dubai's Property Market 120
   2. Tokyo's Housing Stability 120
Practical Applications: Leveraging Global Markets 121
   For Investors 121
   For Developers 121
   For Buyers 121
Conclusion: The World at Your Doorstep 122

Chapter 10: The Drivers of Future Trends in Real Estate 123
   1. Technology and Innovation 123
   2. Sustainability and Green Development. 124
   3. Demographic Shifts 125
   4. Globalization and Cross-Border Investments 126
Emerging Trends in Real Estate Development 127
   1. Mixed-Use Developments 127
   2. Smart Cities 127
   3. Affordable Housing Innovations 127
   4. Remote Work and Suburbanization 128
Predictions for Future Real Estate Markets 129
   1. Increased Digitalization 129
   2. Greater Focus on Wellness 129
   3. Decentralized Urbanization 129
Asset-Backed Mortgages and Future Financing Innovations 130

Opportunities in Future Real Estate Markets..131
Practical Case Studies......................................132
    1. The Rise of Vertical Cities.....................132
    2. Africa's Urban Boom 132
Conclusion: The Road Ahead 133
Chapter 11: Final Thoughts and Summary 134
Key Lessons from the Journey 135
    1. Understanding Market Dynamics..........135
    2. The Power of Location 136
    3. Valuation as a Strategic Tool 136
    4. Navigating Global Real Estate Markets 137
    5. The Role of Innovation..........................138
Six Practical Next Steps for Moving Forward .139
    1. Stay Informed..139
    2. Analyze Opportunities...........................139
    3. Think Long-Term...................................139
    4. Diversify Your Portfolio 140
    5. Leverage Professional Networks 140
    6. Embrace Technology 140
The Future of Real Estate Economics 141
Conclusion: Building Your Real Estate Roadmap
....142
Chapter 12: Conclusion and Call to Action............143
Glossary of Key Words 148
Additional Advanced Terms..154
Acknowledgements 156
Social Profiles 159
Mentorship, Coaching, Consulting and Public Speaking...160

About the Author **162**
List of Books to Date **164**
    Real Estate Mastery Books Series 167
We Value your Feedback **168**
    Portfolio of Books by Willem Tait 169

Chapter 1: Introduction to Real Estate Economics

Real estate is far more than bricks and mortar. It is a living, breathing part of our world, connecting people, communities, and economies.

Whether it's the towering skyscrapers of city centers, sprawling suburban neighborhoods, or the quiet countryside estates, real estate is woven into the fabric of our everyday lives. But have you ever stopped to consider the economic engine that drives it all?

Understanding real estate economics isn't just for industry professionals or wealthy investors. It's for anyone curious about how the places we live, work, and play are shaped, and how they shape us in return.

This chapter will take you on a journey through the fundamentals of real estate economics, providing a foundation for what's to come in this book. By the time you finish reading, you'll have a new appreciation for the forces that shape the real estate world and their impact on our daily lives.

Now, let's start with an intriguing thought: what if you could look at your surroundings, a high-rise apartment, a bustling shopping mall, or even a vacant plot of land, and see the invisible forces at work behind it all?

Forces like supply and demand, government policies, and market cycles. These are the threads that weave together the story of real estate economics, and they're what we'll unravel in the pages ahead.

What Is Real Estate Economics?

At its core, real estate economics is the study of how people interact with land and property in the context of economic principles.

It answers questions like:

- Why do property values rise and fall?
- What causes housing shortages or surpluses?
- How do interest rates and government policies influence the real estate market?

These questions are not just academic, they have real-world implications for homeowners, renters, investors, and governments alike.

Real estate economics blends two powerful disciplines: real estate, which focuses on the ownership, development, and management of property, and economics, the study of how resources are allocated.

Together, they create a lens through which we can understand the complexities of property markets, from local neighborhoods to global real estate trends.

For example, have you ever noticed how housing prices in a city like New York or London seem to defy gravity, climbing higher and higher?

Or have you considered how a new infrastructure project, like a railway station, can suddenly make a once-quiet suburb the hottest market in town?

These phenomena are not random; they're rooted in the principles of real estate economics.

Real Estate and Economics

Why does real estate economics matter? The answer lies in its impact on both individuals and societies.

For Individuals:

Whether you're buying your first home, investing in rental properties, or even just renting an apartment, understanding real estate economics gives you an edge. It helps you make informed decisions, anticipate market trends, and avoid costly mistakes.

For example, knowing how interest rates affect mortgage costs can help you time your property purchase more effectively.

For Societies:

On a broader scale, real estate is a cornerstone of economic growth and stability.

It's one of the largest sectors in most economies, influencing everything from employment to consumer spending. Real estate markets also serve as a barometer for economic health; a booming property market often signals confidence, while a downturn can be an early warning sign of recession.

Governments rely on real estate economics to shape housing policies, plan urban development, and allocate resources efficiently. It's not just about building homes; it's about building communities that thrive.

Five Key Real Estate Economic Concepts

To truly understand real estate economics, you need to grasp a few fundamental concepts. These will serve as the building blocks for everything we'll explore in this book.

1. Supply and Demand

This is the cornerstone of any economic system, and real estate is no exception. When demand for property exceeds supply, prices go up. Conversely, when there's a surplus of properties, prices tend to fall.

Understanding these dynamics is crucial for anyone involved in real estate.

2. Market Cycles

Real estate markets are cyclical, going through phases of growth, stability, and decline. Recognising where we are in the cycle can help investors and policymakers make smarter decisions.

3. Location

The old adage "location, location, location" holds true. Proximity to amenities, schools, transport, and employment opportunities can significantly impact property values.

But location isn't static; it evolves with infrastructure development and urban planning.

4. Government Policies

From zoning laws to tax incentives, government policies play a pivotal role in shaping real estate markets. A single policy change can make or break a market, which is why staying informed is critical.

5. Interest Rates

Interest rates affect borrowing costs, which in turn influence property affordability. When rates are low, borrowing is cheaper, often driving up demand and prices.

High rates usually have the opposite effect.

Why Real Estate Economics Matter

Imagine this scenario: You buy a home, thinking it's the perfect investment.

A year later, property values in your area plummet because a major employer relocates, causing job losses and an exodus of residents. If you'd understood the economic underpinnings of your local real estate market, could you have anticipated this?

Or consider this: You're an investor eyeing a trendy neighborhood, only to find out later that new regulations will cap rental rates, slashing your potential profits. Again, understanding the economic environment could have saved you from disappointment.

These stories aren't meant to scare you; they're meant to show you the power of knowledge.

By understanding real estate economics, you can navigate the market with confidence, whether you're a first-time buyer, a seasoned investor, or simply someone curious about how the world around you works.

Preparing for the Journey Ahead

This book isn't just about theory; it's about practical insights you can apply in real life.

Over the next chapters, we'll delve deeper into the economic indicators that shape real estate markets, explore the forces of supply and demand, and demystify the impact of interest rates, government policies, and global trends.

We'll also look at real-world case studies to illustrate these concepts, from the housing booms and busts of the past to the challenges and opportunities of today's market.

By the end, you'll not only understand real estate economics, you'll see the world through its lens.

So, if you're ready to unlock the secrets of real estate economics, turn the page. The journey starts here, and I promise, it's one worth taking.

Chapter 2: Economic Indicators and Real Estate Markets

Real estate is deeply intertwined with the broader economy. It doesn't exist in isolation; it rises, falls, and shifts alongside economic trends.

Understanding this connection is essential for anyone who wants to navigate the real estate market with confidence.

At the heart of this interplay are economic indicators, those vital signs of an economy that help us predict market behavior, gauge investment potential, and make informed decisions.

Economic indicators aren't just abstract statistics. They're the pulse of the economy, influencing everything from housing prices to rental demand.

This chapter will explore key economic indicators and their impact on real estate markets, offering you a practical framework to interpret these signals and apply them to your real estate decisions.

Let's start with a powerful idea: what if you could predict a property market boom or bust simply by watching the news?

What if the unemployment rate, inflation figures, or GDP growth could give you a heads-up about where the market is headed?

That's the value of understanding economic indicators, they act as a crystal ball, helping you see the road ahead.

What Are Economic Indicators?

Economic indicators are data points or statistics that provide insights into the health of an economy.

Governments, economists, and analysts track these indicators to understand trends and make policy or investment decisions. For real estate, these indicators play a pivotal role in shaping demand, supply, and prices.

Broadly, economic indicators fall into three categories:

1. Leading Indicators: These signal future economic activity. Examples include building permits and stock market performance.
2. Lagging Indicators: These reflect past economic performance, such as unemployment rates.
3. Coincident Indicators: These occur in real-time, like retail sales and GDP.

Each type of indicator provides a unique piece of the puzzle, and together, they paint a comprehensive picture of the economy, and the real estate market.

Key Economic Indicators and Their Impact on Real Estate

1. Gross Domestic Product (GDP)

GDP measures the total value of goods and services produced within a country. It's the ultimate measure of economic health. When GDP is growing, it indicates a strong economy, often leading to increased demand for real estate. People feel confident about their financial stability, which drives home-buying, construction, and investment.

However, during periods of GDP contraction, the opposite occurs. A shrinking economy means fewer jobs, lower consumer spending, and reduced demand for property.

Take the global financial crisis of 2008 as an example. A significant GDP decline led to a sharp drop in real estate transactions and property values, highlighting how closely GDP and real estate are linked.

2. Inflation

Inflation, the rate at which prices for goods and services rise, has a complex relationship with real estate. On one hand, inflation increases the cost of construction materials, pushing up property prices.

On the other hand, real estate often acts as a hedge against inflation because property values tend to rise in line with overall price increases.

For buyers and investors, inflation can be a double-edged sword. Higher prices mean higher investment costs, but they also signal potential for long-term gains. Understanding inflation's impact on affordability and investment returns is key to making smart decisions in real estate markets.

3. Employment Rates

Employment levels are a crucial indicator of economic health, and a direct driver of real estate demand. When employment is high, people have stable incomes, which boosts confidence in buying or renting property.

Conversely, high unemployment can lead to reduced demand for housing, falling property prices, and higher vacancy rates in rental markets. For landlords and investors, keeping an eye on employment trends in specific regions can help identify opportunities or risks.

4. Interest Rates

Interest rates determine the cost of borrowing, making them one of the most influential factors in real estate. Lower interest rates make mortgages more affordable, encouraging home-buying and investment. Higher rates, however, can cool demand by increasing monthly repayments.

Central banks often adjust interest rates to control inflation or stimulate economic growth. For real estate professionals, understanding these shifts can provide valuable insights into market conditions.

5. Housing Starts and Building Permits

Housing starts refer to the number of new residential construction projects that begin in a given period, while building permits indicate the volume of approved construction plans. These are powerful leading indicators of real estate supply.

When housing starts and permits increase, it signals confidence in the market and a growing supply of properties. A decline, however, may indicate caution among developers, often due to economic uncertainty or lower demand.

Interpreting Economic Indicators

Economic indicators don't exist in isolation, they interact with each other and influence real estate markets in complex ways.

For example, high GDP growth might lead to rising employment and wages, which boosts demand for property. But if inflation rises alongside, it could push up construction costs, limiting supply.

Successful real estate investors and professionals understand these dynamics and use them to make strategic decisions. They look for patterns, ask critical questions, and adapt their strategies to align with economic realities.

Here's an example: Imagine you're considering investing in a rental property. The unemployment rate in the area is low, and GDP is growing steadily. However, inflation is high, driving up property prices.

By understanding these indicators, you might decide to move forward cautiously, ensuring your rental income can cover potential cost increases.

A Real-World Application: Economic Indicators in Action

Let's consider a case study: the U.S. housing market during the COVID-19 pandemic.

- GDP: In the early months of the pandemic, GDP contracted sharply, signaling economic distress.
- Employment: Unemployment spiked, reducing demand for rental properties in urban areas as people moved to more affordable locations.
- Interest Rates: The Federal Reserve slashed interest rates to near-zero levels, making mortgages incredibly cheap and fueling a housing boom.
- Building Permits: A surge in demand for suburban homes led to an increase in building permits and housing starts.

By tracking these indicators, real estate professionals could anticipate shifts in demand, adapt their strategies, and seize opportunities in a rapidly changing market.

The Importance of Staying Informed

Economic indicators are constantly evolving, reflecting the ever-changing nature of the economy.

Staying informed about these shifts is essential for anyone involved in real estate, whether you're a buyer, seller, investor, or policymaker.

In today's world, access to economic data is easier than ever. From government reports to financial news platforms, the information is readily available.

The challenge lies in interpreting it correctly and applying it to your real estate decisions.

Conclusion: Reading the Signs

Economic indicators are like signposts on the road to real estate success.

They point the way, warn of potential dangers, and guide you toward informed decisions. By understanding GDP, inflation, employment rates, interest rates, and housing starts, you can navigate the real estate market with confidence.

Here's a final thought to keep you turning the pages: What if the next housing boom or bust could be predicted not by chance, but by knowledge? The chapters ahead will explore more of these hidden forces, from supply and demand dynamics to global trends.

Keep reading to uncover the tools and insights that will empower you in the world of real estate economics.

Chapter 3: Supply and Demand Dynamics

The real estate market, like all markets, thrives on the delicate balance of supply and demand.

These two forces are at the core of real estate economics, determining property prices, influencing market trends, and shaping investment opportunities.

Whether you're a first-time buyer, a seasoned investor, or simply someone curious about real estate, understanding supply and demand dynamics is essential to navigating the market with confidence.

This chapter delves into the intricacies of supply and demand in real estate, exploring the factors that influence them and their interplay.

Along the way, we'll prepare you for the deeper dives into market cycles, government policies, and global trends that follow in later chapters.

But first, here's something to consider:

- Why do property prices in some cities skyrocket while others stagnate?
- What makes one neighborhood flourish while another fades?

The answers lie in the dynamic push and pull of supply and demand.

The Fundamentals of Supply and Demand in Real Estate

At its most basic, supply refers to the availability of properties in the market, while demand represents the desire and ability of buyers to purchase those properties.

When demand exceeds supply, prices rise, a phenomenon known as a seller's market. Conversely, when supply outpaces demand, prices fall, creating a buyer's market.

Real estate is unique because it is inherently local. Supply and demand dynamics can vary significantly between cities, neighborhoods, or even streets.

This localized nature makes understanding these dynamics both an art and a science.

Factors Influencing Supply

Supply in real estate isn't as straightforward as simply building more properties.

It's shaped by a variety of factors, many of which are outside an individual's control.

1. Land Availability

Land is a finite resource, and its availability is a key determinant of supply. In densely populated urban areas, limited land drives up property prices.

In contrast, rural or suburban areas with abundant land often have a more balanced supply.

For example, cities like Hong Kong and Tokyo face chronic land shortages, leading to some of the highest property prices in the world.

As we'll explore in future chapters on urban economics, land scarcity creates unique challenges and opportunities for real estate markets.

2. Construction Costs

The cost of building materials, labor, and regulatory compliance directly impacts the supply of real estate. When construction costs rise, developers may delay or cancel projects, reducing the number of new properties entering the market.

3. Government Policies and Regulations

Zoning laws, building permits, and taxation policies can either encourage or hinder new developments. For instance, restrictive zoning laws can limit housing supply, driving up prices. Later chapters will dive deeper into the role of government in shaping real estate markets.

4. Market Cycles

The real estate market is cyclical, with periods of growth, stability, and decline. During a downturn, developers may scale back construction, reducing supply. Conversely, in a booming market, construction activity often surges. Understanding these cycles, which we'll explore in Chapter 4, is crucial for anticipating supply changes.

Factors Influencing Demand

Demand is driven by the needs and desires of buyers, but it's also influenced by broader economic and social factors.

1. Population Growth

As populations grow, so does the need for housing. Urbanization, where people move from rural areas to cities, can create intense demand in urban markets.

For instance, rapid urbanization in cities like Mumbai and Lagos has led to significant housing shortages, driving up prices and spurring innovative housing solutions.

2. Income Levels and Employment

Higher income levels and stable employment fuel demand by increasing buyers' purchasing power. When people feel financially secure, they're more likely to invest in property.

3. Interest Rates

As discussed in Chapter 2, interest rates play a pivotal role in real estate demand. Low rates make borrowing cheaper, encouraging buyers to enter the market. High rates, on the other hand, can dampen demand by increasing mortgage costs.

4. Consumer Confidence

Real estate purchases are significant financial decisions often influenced by confidence in the economy. During periods of economic uncertainty, demand may decrease as buyers adopt a wait-and-see approach.

The Interplay Between Supply and Demand

Supply and demand don't operate in isolation; they are constantly interacting, influencing each other and shaping the real estate market.

1. Supply Shortages and Price Increases

When supply is constrained, whether due to land scarcity, high construction costs, or regulatory barriers, prices tend to rise.

This is often seen in urban markets with high population densities and limited development opportunities.

2. Oversupply and Price Drops

Conversely, when there is an oversupply of properties, often due to overbuilding during a market boom, prices can fall.

This can create opportunities for buyers but challenges for sellers and developers.

3. Elasticity in Real Estate Markets

Real estate markets are often considered inelastic, meaning that supply cannot quickly adjust to changes in demand. Unlike consumer goods, building new properties takes time, sometimes years, making the market slower to respond to demand shifts.

Real Estate Sectoral Dynamics

The dynamics of supply and demand vary across different real estate sectors, each with its own unique drivers.

Residential Real Estate

Residential markets are heavily influenced by population trends, income levels, and lifestyle changes. For instance, the rise of remote work has increased demand for suburban and rural homes, reshaping traditional patterns of urban housing demand.

Commercial Real Estate

Commercial markets are tied to business activity and economic growth.

A booming economy drives demand for office spaces, retail properties, and warehouses, while an economic downturn can lead to increased vacancies and falling rents.

Industrial Real Estate

The industrial sector is influenced by global trade, e-commerce, and logistics.

For example, the surge in online shopping has driven demand for warehouses and distribution centers, reshaping industrial real estate dynamics.

Practical Applications: Using Supply and Demand to Your Advantage

Understanding supply and demand dynamics can help you make smarter real estate decisions, whether you're buying, selling, or investing.

- Investors: Look for markets where demand is outpacing supply, indicating potential for price growth.
- Homebuyers: Consider supply constraints in your target area, as they can drive long-term value appreciation.
- Developers: Monitor demand trends to identify underserved markets and capitalize on opportunities.

As we explore future chapters, you'll gain even more tools to analyze these dynamics and apply them to real-world scenarios.

A Real-World Case Study: The California Housing Crisis

California's housing market is a textbook example of supply and demand dynamics.

- Supply Constraints: Limited land availability, strict zoning laws, and high construction costs have constrained housing supply.
- Demand Drivers: Population growth, high income levels, and urbanization have fueled intense demand.
- Result: A chronic housing shortage has led to skyrocketing prices, making homeownership unattainable for many.

This case underscores the importance of addressing both supply and demand factors to create a balanced market.

Conclusion: The Balancing Act

Supply and demand dynamics are the heartbeat of the real estate market, shaping everything from property prices to investment opportunities.

By understanding the factors that influence these dynamics, you can navigate the market with greater confidence and insight.

But this is just the beginning. In the next chapter, we'll explore market cycles, those predictable yet often misunderstood patterns that govern real estate markets over time.

Understanding these cycles will help you anticipate changes and stay ahead of the curve.

So, turn the page and continue your journey into the fascinating world of real estate economics.

The more you learn, the better equipped you'll be to seize opportunities and avoid pitfalls in this ever-evolving market.

Chapter 4: Market Cycles and Trends

Real estate markets, much like the broader economy, move in cycles. These cycles can bring periods of prosperity, stability, and even decline. For anyone involved in real estate, whether as a buyer, seller, investor, or developer, understanding these cycles is critical to making informed decisions and seizing opportunities.

Market cycles don't just happen by chance. They are influenced by a combination of economic, social, and psychological factors that create patterns over time. Recognizing these patterns and predicting trends can give you an edge in navigating the ever-changing real estate landscape.

In this chapter, we'll explore the fascinating world of market cycles and trends, building on the foundation of supply and demand dynamics discussed in Chapter 3. By the end, you'll not only understand the phases of market cycles but also see how they connect to economic indicators (from Chapter 2) and set the stage for government policies and global market dynamics, which we'll explore in future chapters.

The Nature of Market Cycles

Market cycles are recurring periods of growth, stability, and decline within a real estate market.

These cycles are influenced by economic conditions, consumer behavior, and even geopolitical events. While no two cycles are identical, they share common phases:

1. Expansion

This phase is marked by increasing demand, rising property prices, and active construction. Economic indicators like GDP growth, low unemployment, and rising consumer confidence often signal the start of an expansion. Developers respond to high demand by launching new projects, and investors flock to the market, anticipating strong returns.

2. Peak

As the market reaches its peak, property prices are at their highest, and supply begins to outpace demand. Signs of overbuilding may appear, and affordability becomes a concern for buyers. The peak phase often precedes a slowdown, making it a critical time for cautious decision-making.

3. Contraction

During this phase, demand slows, property prices level off or decline, and vacancy rates increase. Economic uncertainty or rising interest rates can trigger this phase, discouraging new investments and construction activity.

4. Trough

The trough is the lowest point in the cycle, characterized by stagnant or declining prices, low construction activity, and a buyer's market. However, it also presents opportunities for savvy investors to purchase properties at discounted prices, setting the stage for the next expansion.

Factors Driving Market Cycles

Market cycles are shaped by a combination of supply and demand dynamics, economic indicators, and external influences. Here's a closer look at the key drivers:

1. Economic Conditions

As discussed in Chapter 2, economic indicators like GDP, employment rates, and interest rates play a significant role in shaping market cycles.

For instance, strong GDP growth often fuels demand, driving an expansion phase, while economic downturns can trigger contractions.

2. Consumer Behavior

Psychological factors, such as consumer confidence and market sentiment, influence buying and selling decisions.

For example, during periods of economic optimism, buyers are more willing to invest in property, fueling demand and driving up prices.

3. Government Policies

Policies like tax incentives, interest rate adjustments, and zoning regulations can influence market cycles.

For example, government initiatives to promote affordable housing may stimulate demand in lower-income segments, creating localized expansions. Chapter 6 will explore these policy influences in greater detail.

4. Global Events

Geopolitical events, natural disasters, and pandemics can disrupt market cycles, creating unpredictable trends.

For instance, the COVID-19 pandemic reshaped housing demand, accelerating trends like remote work and suburban migration.

Identifying the Four Real Estate Market Trends

Market trends are the observable patterns within a cycle that provide insights into current and future market conditions.

Identifying these trends requires analyzing both quantitative data and qualitative factors.

1. Demographic Trends

Population growth, aging populations, and migration patterns influence demand for housing.

For example, the rise of millennials entering the housing market has driven demand for starter homes in many regions.

2. Technological Advancements

Technology impacts how properties are built, marketed, and sold.

Trends like smart homes, virtual tours, and online real estate platforms have transformed the industry, creating new opportunities and challenges.

3. Sustainability and Green Building

Environmental awareness has led to a growing demand for energy-efficient and sustainable properties.

This trend is likely to intensify in the coming years, as discussed in future chapters on global real estate markets.

4. Urbanization and Suburbanization

Urbanization drives demand in city centers, while suburbanization, accelerated by remote work trends, shifts demand to outer suburbs and rural areas.

These opposing forces create unique opportunities in different markets.

Predicting Three Market Cycles and Trends

While no one can predict the future with absolute certainty, understanding market cycles and analyzing trends can help you anticipate changes and make better decisions.

1. Analyzing Historical Data

Historical data provides valuable insights into how markets have behaved in the past, offering clues about future cycles. For example, examining the aftermath of the 2008 financial crisis can help us understand how markets recover from downturns.

2. Monitoring Leading Indicators

As discussed in Chapter 2, leading economic indicators like building permits and consumer sentiment can signal upcoming changes in the market.

3. Staying Informed

Keeping up with industry reports, news, and expert analyses is essential for identifying emerging trends. As we'll explore in Chapter 10, staying ahead of future trends is key to thriving in the ever-changing real estate landscape.

Practical Applications: Navigating Market Cycles

Understanding market cycles isn't just theoretical, it has practical applications for buyers, sellers, and investors alike.

For Buyers:

Recognizing a market's position in the cycle can help you decide whether to buy now or wait for better opportunities.

For Sellers:

Timing your sale during the peak phase can maximize your return, while selling during a contraction may require strategic pricing.

For Investors:

Identifying opportunities in the trough phase can yield significant returns as the market moves into expansion.

By applying these insights, you can make smarter, more strategic decisions in real estate markets.

Real-World Case Study: The 2008 Financial Crisis

The global financial crisis of 2008 is a powerful example of how market cycles can impact real estate.

- Expansion: Prior to the crisis, low interest rates and high consumer confidence fueled a housing boom.
- Peak: By 2006, the market had reached its peak, with property prices soaring and speculative investments increasing.
- Contraction: The collapse of subprime mortgages triggered a market contraction, leading to widespread foreclosures and falling property values.
- Trough: The market hit bottom in 2009, creating opportunities for investors to buy distressed properties at discounted prices.

This case highlights the importance of understanding market cycles and the risks of ignoring warning signs.

Conclusion: Timing Is Everything

Market cycles and trends are the heartbeat of the real estate market, offering both challenges and opportunities.

By understanding the phases of a cycle, the factors driving them, and the trends shaping the market, you can navigate the real estate landscape with confidence.

As we move into the next chapters, we'll explore the impact of government policies on real estate markets and dive into the dynamics of global real estate trends.

These insights will build on what you've learned about market cycles, giving you a comprehensive understanding of real estate economics.

So, stay with us as we continue this journey into the fascinating world of real estate economics.

The more you learn, the more empowered you'll be to succeed in this dynamic and ever-changing market.

Chapter 5: The Impact of Interest Rates

Interest rates are one of the most powerful forces shaping real estate markets.

These seemingly simple percentages wield tremendous influence over property values, investment decisions, and market trends. Whether you're buying your first home, managing a portfolio of properties, or considering a large-scale development project, understanding how interest rates work, and how they impact real estate, is essential.

This chapter examines the role of interest rates in real estate economics, building on the foundations of economic indicators (Chapter 2), supply and demand dynamics (Chapter 3), and market cycles (Chapter 4).

As we progress, we'll explore their impact on property values, mortgage affordability, and long-term investment strategies. We'll also set the stage for discussions on government policies and future trends in later chapters.

What Are Interest Rates?

Interest rates are the cost of borrowing money, typically expressed as a percentage of the loan amount.

They are determined by central banks, such as the Federal Reserve in the United States or the European Central Bank, as part of monetary policy. Interest rates influence everything from consumer loans to corporate financing, and, of course, real estate markets.

In real estate, interest rates affect the cost of mortgages, which are the primary way most people finance property purchases.

When rates are low, borrowing is cheaper, making property more affordable and attractive to buyers.

Conversely, high interest rates increase borrowing costs, reducing affordability and cooling demand.

The Connection Between Interest Rates and Real Estate

The relationship between interest rates and real estate is complex, dynamic, and multi-faceted. To fully appreciate this connection, let's explore its impact on key aspects of the market.

1. Property Values

Interest rates directly affect property values by influencing buyers' purchasing power.

- Low Interest Rates: When rates are low, buyers can afford larger loans, increasing their purchasing power. This often drives up property prices as more buyers compete for limited inventory.
- High Interest Rates: Higher rates reduce purchasing power, limiting what buyers can afford and putting downward pressure on property prices.

For example, during the early 2020s, historically low interest rates contributed to a global housing boom, with property prices surging in many markets. As rates began to rise in subsequent years, those same markets experienced a cooling effect, demonstrating the direct link between interest rates and property values.

2. Mortgage Affordability

Mortgages are the lifeblood of residential real estate markets, and their affordability is closely tied to interest rates.

- Lower Monthly Payments: Lower rates mean lower monthly mortgage payments, making homeownership accessible to more people.
- Higher Monthly Payments: When rates rise, monthly payments increase, pricing some buyers out of the market.

This dynamic can also impact refinancing decisions. Homeowners with higher-rate mortgages may seek to refinance when rates drop, reducing their monthly payments and freeing up disposable income.

3. Investment Decisions

Interest rates play a pivotal role in shaping real estate investment strategies.

- Low Rates: Investors often flock to real estate during periods of low interest rates, attracted by cheaper financing and the potential for higher returns.
- High Rates: Rising rates can deter investment by increasing borrowing costs and compressing profit margins.

Later in this book, we'll delve deeper into how investors navigate these challenges, particularly in commercial and industrial real estate sectors.

The Broader Economic Impact

Interest rates don't just influence individual buyers and investors.

Rates ripple through the broader economy, creating feedback loops that further impact real estate markets.

1. Consumer Spending

When rates are low, consumers have more disposable income, boosting spending on goods, services, and home improvements.

High rates, however, tighten budgets, leading to reduced economic activity.

2. Construction Activity

Developers are highly sensitive to interest rates, as they rely on financing to fund projects. Low rates encourage construction, increasing supply in the market.

High rates, on the other hand, can stall projects, limiting supply and potentially driving up prices.

3. Employment Trends

Real estate-related industries, such as construction and mortgage lending, are significant employers.

Changes in interest rates can influence job creation or losses in these sectors, further affecting local economies and housing markets.

Historical Examples of Interest Rate Impacts

The Early 2000s Housing Boom

In the early 2000s, low interest rates fueled a housing boom in many countries, including the United States. Buyers rushed into the market, driving up prices and spurring rapid construction.

However, this boom also contributed to the subprime mortgage crisis, demonstrating the risks of overreliance on cheap credit.

The COVID-19 Pandemic

During the COVID-19 pandemic, central banks worldwide slashed interest rates to stimulate economic activity. This led to a surge in demand for housing as buyers capitalized on low mortgage rates.

The resulting price increases underscored the significant influence of interest rates on real estate markets.

Predicting Interest Rate Trends

Predicting interest rate trends is a challenging but essential part of real estate strategy. Here are some key factors to consider:

1. Central Bank Policies

Central banks adjust interest rates based on economic conditions, such as inflation and unemployment. Monitoring central bank announcements can provide insights into future rate changes.

2. Global Economic Conditions

Interest rates are influenced by global economic trends, such as trade dynamics, currency fluctuations, and geopolitical events. Staying informed about these factors can help you anticipate rate movements.

3. Market Sentiment

Investor sentiment and consumer confidence also play a role in shaping interest rate expectations. For example, markets may price in anticipated rate hikes or cuts, influencing borrowing costs even before official changes occur.

Practical Applications: Navigating Interest Rate Impacts

Understanding the impact of interest rates can help you make smarter decisions in real estate markets.

- For Homebuyers: Consider locking in fixed-rate mortgages during periods of low interest rates to protect against future increases.
- For Investors: Evaluate the cost of financing against potential returns, and consider alternative strategies during high-rate environments.
- For Developers: Plan projects strategically, taking into account potential rate changes and their impact on financing and demand.

As we'll explore in Chapter 7 on property valuation, interest rates also influence appraisal methods, adding another layer of complexity to real estate decision-making.

A Real-World Case Study: The UK Housing Market

The United Kingdom provides a compelling example of how interest rates shape real estate markets.

- Low Rates: Following the 2008 financial crisis, the Bank of England slashed interest rates to historic lows, spurring a housing recovery.
- Rising Rates: In the early 2020s, rising inflation prompted rate hikes, cooling demand and slowing price growth.
- Impact on Buyers and Sellers: These shifts created challenges for first-time buyers, who faced affordability issues, and sellers, who struggled to maintain property values.

This case highlights the importance of adapting to changing interest rate environments.

Conclusion: The Power of Percentages

Interest rates may seem like small numbers, but their impact on real estate markets is monumental.

From influencing property values to shaping investment strategies, these rates are a cornerstone of real estate economics.

As we move into the next chapters, we'll explore the role of government policies in real estate markets (Chapter 6) and delve into property valuation methods (Chapter 7).

These discussions will build on your understanding of interest rates, offering new tools and insights to navigate the complexities of real estate.

The more you learn, the better equipped you'll be to make confident, informed decisions in this ever-changing market.

So, turn the page and continue your journey.

Chapter 6: Government Policies and Regulations

Government policies and regulations are the invisible hands that shape the real estate market.

While interest rates (discussed in Chapter 5) or supply and demand dynamics (Chapter 3) may dominate headlines, it's government actions that often have the most profound and lasting effects on real estate.

From zoning laws to tax policies, these rules dictate what can be built, where it can be built, and how it can be bought or sold.

Understanding the role of government in real estate is crucial for anyone looking to navigate this complex landscape. Policies can create opportunities, but they can also impose challenges.

Whether you're a buyer, investor, or developer, knowing how regulations influence the market will empower you to make informed decisions.

This chapter explores how government policies and regulations shape real estate markets, building on the foundations laid in previous chapters.

We'll discuss their impact on property values, investment decisions, and market trends, while also setting the stage for future chapters on valuation methods and global trends.

The Role of Government

Governments play a dual role in real estate: as regulators and as participants.

1. Regulators

Governments establish laws and policies that govern how real estate markets operate. These regulations can influence everything from housing supply to transaction costs.

For example, zoning laws dictate land use, determining whether an area can be developed for residential, commercial, or industrial purposes.

Tax policies, on the other hand, affect affordability by influencing the cost of property ownership.

2. Participants

Governments also participate in real estate markets by building infrastructure, subsidizing housing, or directly owning and managing properties. These actions can have a ripple effect on property values and market dynamics.

Key Areas of Government Impact

Government policies and regulations influence real estate in several critical areas:

1. Zoning and Land Use Regulations

Zoning laws are one of the most visible ways governments shape real estate markets. These regulations dictate what types of buildings can be constructed in specific areas, as well as their height, density, and usage.

- Residential Zones: Restrict development to housing, limiting commercial activity.
- Commercial Zones: Encourage business activity, creating demand for office and retail spaces.
- Mixed-Use Zones: Combine residential, commercial, and recreational spaces, fostering vibrant communities.

Zoning laws can impact supply and demand dynamics, as discussed in Chapter 3. For instance, restrictive zoning in urban areas can limit housing supply, driving up prices.

2. Tax Policies

Taxes are another powerful tool governments use to influence real estate markets. These include:

- Property Taxes: Levied annually on property owners, these taxes fund public services like schools and infrastructure. High property taxes can discourage homeownership, while tax incentives can attract investors.
- Capital Gains Taxes: Applied to profits from property sales, these taxes can influence investment strategies. Lower rates may encourage property flipping, while higher rates may promote long-term ownership.
- Transfer Taxes: Charged during property transactions, these can increase the cost of buying or selling real estate.

3. Affordable Housing Initiatives

Many governments implement policies to promote affordable housing, addressing inequalities in the market. These initiatives may include:

- Subsidized Housing: Government-built or -funded housing for low-income families.
- Rent Control: Regulations that cap rent increases to protect tenants from market volatility.

- Inclusionary Zoning: Requirements for developers to include affordable housing units in new projects.

While these policies aim to improve access to housing, they can also impact supply and demand dynamics by discouraging development in some cases.

4. Infrastructure Development

Infrastructure projects, such as highways, airports, and public transit systems, have a significant impact on real estate markets. Improved accessibility can increase property values in surrounding areas, attracting both buyers and investors.

For example, the construction of a new metro line can transform a previously overlooked suburb into a sought-after location. This interplay between infrastructure and property values ties back to concepts discussed in Chapter 4 on market cycles and trends.

5. Environmental Regulations

Sustainability is becoming a central focus of real estate development. Governments are introducing regulations to promote energy efficiency, reduce carbon emissions, and protect natural resources.

- Building Codes: Mandate energy-efficient materials and designs.
- Green Incentives: Offer tax breaks or subsidies for sustainable developments.
- Land Preservation: Restrict development in environmentally sensitive areas.

These policies not only shape the supply of properties but also influence consumer preferences and investment strategies.

How Policy Changes Affect Real Estate

Government policies are not static, they evolve in response to economic, social, and political pressures.

These changes can create both opportunities and risks in real estate markets.

1. Economic Stimulus Measures

During economic downturns, governments often implement stimulus measures to revive real estate markets. These may include:

- Lowering Interest Rates: As discussed in Chapter 5, this makes borrowing cheaper and boosts demand.
- Tax Breaks for Buyers: Encourage homeownership by reducing upfront costs.
- Subsidies for Developers: Incentivize construction to increase housing supply.

2. Regulatory Tightening

Conversely, governments may introduce stricter regulations to address market imbalances or prevent speculative bubbles. Examples include:

- Loan-to-Value (LTV) Limits: Restrict the amount buyers can borrow relative to property value.
- Foreign Buyer Taxes: Discourage overseas investors from inflating local markets.
- Anti-Speculation Measures: Penalize short-term property flipping.

3. Political Changes

Elections and shifts in political leadership can bring significant policy changes, impacting real estate markets. For instance, a government focused on housing affordability may prioritize rent controls, while a pro-business administration might reduce taxes to attract investment.

Historical Examples of Policy Impact on Real Estate

1. Singapore's Cooling Measures

In the early 2010s, Singapore introduced a series of measures to cool its overheated property market, including higher stamp duties for foreign buyers and stricter loan limits. These policies successfully reduced speculative activity, stabilizing prices and promoting long-term investment.

2. The U.S. New Deal

During the Great Depression, the U.S. government launched the New Deal, which included programs to build affordable housing and provide loans to struggling homeowners. These initiatives helped revive the housing market and laid the groundwork for modern real estate policies.

Practical Applications: Navigating Government Policies

Understanding government policies and regulations is essential for success in real estate markets.

- For Homebuyers: Stay informed about tax incentives or subsidies that can reduce costs.
- For Investors: Monitor policy changes that may affect rental yields or capital appreciation.
- For Developers: Plan projects with zoning laws, environmental regulations, and market demand in mind.

Future chapters will explore how these policies intersect with valuation methods (Chapter 7) and global market trends (Chapter 9), offering deeper insights into their impact.

Conclusion: The Policy Puzzle

Government policies and regulations are a double-edged sword in real estate.

They can create opportunities, but they can also impose challenges. By understanding how these rules shape the market, you can make smarter decisions and adapt to changing conditions.

As we move into the next chapters, we'll delve into property valuation methods and explore the dynamics of global real estate markets.

These discussions will build on the concepts introduced here, offering new tools to navigate the complexities of real estate economics.

So, keep reading. The more you understand the intricate dance between government policies and real estate markets, the better equipped you'll be to thrive in this ever-changing landscape.

Chapter 7: Real Estate Valuation Methods

Real estate is one of the most significant investments many people make, and understanding how properties are valued is crucial.

Whether you're a homeowner, an investor, or a developer, knowing the methods used to determine property values can empower you to make informed decisions. Real estate valuation is not only about calculating a price, it's about understanding the market, future potential, and the factors that influence value.

This chapter will explore the most common methods of valuing real estate properties, why they matter, and how they're applied in different scenarios. We'll also connect these methods to the broader concepts discussed in previous chapters, such as supply and demand dynamics (Chapter 3) and the impact of interest rates (Chapter 5). Looking ahead, you'll see how valuation plays a critical role in understanding urban development (Chapter 8) and navigating global real estate markets (Chapter 9).

Why Real Estate Valuation Matters

Valuation methods provide a systematic way to determine a property's worth. Accurate valuations are essential for several reasons:

- For Buyers and Sellers: Valuations guide pricing decisions, ensuring buyers don't overpay and sellers don't undervalue their property.
- For Investors: Investors rely on valuations to assess potential returns and compare investment opportunities.
- For Lenders: Banks and financial institutions use valuations to determine loan amounts and manage risk.
- For Developers: Valuations help developers estimate project feasibility and potential profitability.

Valuation is also vital for broader market health. Overvalued markets can lead to bubbles, while undervalued markets may signal hidden opportunities.

Key Real Estate Valuation Methods

There are several established methods for valuing real estate, each suited to specific property types and purposes.

1. Sales Comparison Approach (Market Approach)

The sales comparison approach is one of the most widely used methods for valuing residential properties. It involves comparing the subject property to similar properties (comparables or "comps") that have recently sold in the same area.

- Steps in the Sales Comparison Approach:
    - Identify recently sold properties with similar characteristics (location, size, age, etc.).
    - Adjust for differences (e.g., if one property has a pool and another does not).
    - Calculate the estimated value of the subject property based on these adjustments.

This method reflects market trends and buyer preferences, making it highly relevant in markets influenced by supply and demand dynamics

(Chapter 3). However, its accuracy depends on the availability of reliable comparables.

2. Income Approach

The income approach is commonly used for income-generating properties, such as rental buildings, office spaces, or shopping centers. It focuses on the property's potential to generate cash flow.

- Steps in the Income Approach:
    - Estimate the property's net operating income (NOI), calculated as total income minus operating expenses.
    - Apply a capitalization rate (cap rate), which reflects the expected return on investment.
    - Divide the NOI by the cap rate to calculate the property's value.

This method ties directly to economic indicators, such as employment and interest rates (Chapter 2 and Chapter 5), which influence rental income and investor expectations.

3. Cost Approach

The cost approach estimates property value based on the cost to replace or reproduce it.

This method is particularly useful for new constructions or unique properties with few comparables.

- Steps in the Cost Approach:
    - Calculate the cost of constructing the building, including materials, labor, and permits.
    - Subtract depreciation to account for wear and tear.
    - Add the value of the land to arrive at the total property value.

While the cost approach provides a logical valuation, it may not fully account for market conditions or buyer sentiment. It often complements other methods rather than standing alone.

4. Automated Valuation Models (AVMs)

AVMs are increasingly popular in the digital age, using algorithms and large datasets to estimate property values.

These models draw on data from public records, recent sales, and market trends.

- Advantages: Speed and scalability.
- Limitations: Lack of nuance, such as property condition or unique features.

AVMs are transforming the industry and will be discussed further in future chapters on global real estate trends (Chapter 9).

Four Factors Influencing Valuation

While valuation methods provide frameworks, they must account for factors that influence property values.

1. Location

As discussed in Chapter 3, location is one of the most critical determinants of property value. Proximity to schools, transport, and amenities can significantly impact valuations.

2. Market Conditions

Market trends, cycles, and demand levels (Chapter 4) shape valuations. For instance, properties in high-demand areas during an expansion phase are likely to command higher prices.

3. Property Characteristics

Size, age, condition, and unique features (e.g., swimming pools, views) influence a property's value. These characteristics are often accounted for in the sales comparison approach.

4. Economic Indicators

Interest rates, inflation, and employment levels (Chapters 2 and 5) indirectly affect valuations by influencing buyer affordability and investor confidence.

Applying Valuation Methods to Different Property Types

Different property types require tailored valuation approaches.

Residential Properties

The sales comparison approach is most commonly used for residential properties, as it reflects market sentiment and neighborhood trends.

Commercial Properties

The income approach is the standard for commercial real estate, focusing on rental income and investment potential. Cap rates and NOI are central metrics for these properties.

Unique or Special Properties

For properties like historical landmarks or custom-built homes, the cost approach is often the most appropriate, as finding comparables can be challenging.

The Role of Valuation in Urban Economics and Global Markets

Real estate valuation doesn't exist in a vacuum, it plays a critical role in understanding broader trends in urban development and global markets.

Urban Economics and Development

Valuations influence urban planning by determining the feasibility of development projects.

For example, high land values in urban centers may encourage vertical development (e.g., skyscrapers), while lower values in suburban areas may support horizontal growth.

As cities evolve, valuations shift, reflecting changes in infrastructure, zoning laws, and demographic trends.

Chapter 8 will explore how these factors intersect with valuation methods to shape urban landscapes.

Global Real Estate Markets

In global markets, valuation methods must account for currency fluctuations, differing regulatory environments, and cultural preferences.

For instance, what drives value in New York City may differ significantly from what drives value in Tokyo or Dubai.

Chapter 9 will delve into these complexities, providing a global perspective on real estate valuation.

Practical Tips for Applying Valuation Methods

For Buyers and Sellers

- Buyers: Use the sales comparison approach to assess whether a property is fairly priced.
- Sellers: Price your property competitively by analyzing recent sales of similar properties.

For Investors

- Evaluate properties using the income approach, focusing on cap rates and cash flow potential.

For Developers

- Combine the cost approach with market analysis to assess project feasibility and pricing strategies.

Conclusion: Unlocking the Value Puzzle

Real estate valuation is both an art and a science, requiring a blend of established methods and market insights. By understanding the various approaches to valuation, you can make more confident decisions, whether you're buying, selling, or investing.

Looking ahead, Chapter 8 will delve into urban economics and development, showing how valuations shape cities and communities.

From there, Chapter 9 will take us into the global real estate market, exploring how valuation methods adapt to different cultural and economic contexts.

As you continue this journey, remember that valuation is not just about numbers, it's about understanding the forces that drive real estate markets.

The more you learn, the better equipped you'll be to unlock opportunities in this dynamic industry.

Chapter 8: Urban Economics and Development

Cities are the heartbeats of modern economies, serving as hubs of commerce, culture, and innovation.

Urban areas attract millions of people seeking opportunities, shaping the demand for housing, infrastructure, and commercial spaces.

The study of urban economics is crucial to understanding the forces that drive cities and, by extension, their real estate markets.

From the skyscrapers of Manhattan to the sprawling suburbs of Johannesburg, urban economic principles influence every aspect of real estate development.

This chapter explores the intersection of urban economics and real estate, focusing on how urban planning and infrastructure development shape property markets.

Building on the valuation methods discussed in Chapter 7, we'll examine how urban economics informs the value and feasibility of real estate projects.

We'll also set the stage for a global perspective on real estate markets in Chapter 9, as urbanization trends vary widely across regions.

What Is Urban Real Estate Economics?

Urban real estate economics is the study of how cities grow, function, and evolve in response to economic forces.

It examines the distribution of resources, land use, and population density within urban areas.

For real estate professionals, urban economics provides a framework for understanding the factors that influence property values, investment opportunities, and development patterns.

At its core, urban economics revolves around two key questions:

1. How do economic principles shape the growth and structure of cities?
2. How do urban policies and infrastructure decisions affect real estate markets?

The answers lie in the interplay between supply and demand dynamics (Chapter 3), market cycles (Chapter 4), and government regulations (Chapter 6).

The Role of Urban Planning in Real Estate Development

Urban planning is the process of designing and regulating the use of land in cities.

It balances competing interests, such as housing, transportation, and green spaces, to create sustainable and functional urban environments.

1. Land Use and Zoning

Land use planning determines how land is allocated for residential, commercial, industrial, and recreational purposes.

Zoning laws, discussed in Chapter 6, play a critical role in this process by specifying what types of developments are allowed in specific areas.

- Residential Zones: Prioritize housing development, often with density restrictions to maintain neighborhood character.
- Commercial Zones: Encourage business activity, influencing demand for office spaces and retail properties.
- Mixed-Use Zones: Combine housing, workspaces, and amenities, fostering walkable and vibrant communities.

Effective urban planning enhances property values by creating desirable neighborhoods with access to amenities and infrastructure.

2. Infrastructure Development

Infrastructure is the backbone of urban growth, supporting transportation, utilities, and public services.

Real estate development is closely tied to infrastructure investment, as accessibility and connectivity drive demand for properties.

For example, the construction of a new metro line can transform a previously underdeveloped area into a thriving real estate market.

Similarly, investments in roads, airports, and utilities expand the reach of urban development.

3. Sustainability and Smart Cities

Modern urban planning increasingly focuses on sustainability, emphasizing energy-efficient buildings, renewable energy sources, and green spaces.

Smart city initiatives, which integrate technology into urban infrastructure, are reshaping how cities function and how real estate is developed.

As we'll explore in Chapter 9, global trends in sustainability and smart cities are creating new opportunities and challenges for urban real estate markets.

Urbanization and Its Impact on Real Estate

Urbanization, the movement of people from rural areas to cities, is a defining trend of the 21st century.

It drives demand for housing, infrastructure, and commercial spaces, reshaping real estate markets worldwide.

1. Population Growth and Housing Demand

Rapid population growth in urban areas creates intense demand for housing. This demand is often concentrated in city centers, where proximity to jobs and amenities is highest.

However, high land values in urban cores often push development to suburban and peri-urban areas, creating sprawling metropolitan regions.

2. Economic Clusters and Real Estate

Urban areas often develop economic clusters, where businesses in related industries concentrate. These clusters, such as Silicon Valley for tech or Wall Street for finance, drive demand for office spaces, housing, and retail properties.

Economic clusters also influence property values. For instance, neighborhoods near major business hubs typically command premium prices due to their convenience and prestige.

3. Gentrification and Urban Renewal

Gentrification is the process of revitalizing urban neighborhoods, often leading to rising property values and changing demographics.

While gentrification creates investment opportunities, it also raises concerns about affordability and displacement.

Urban renewal initiatives, such as repurposing industrial areas into residential or mixed-use developments, are another aspect of urbanization.

These projects often require significant investment in infrastructure and planning, as discussed in Chapter 7.

Challenges in Urban Development

Urban development faces several challenges that influence real estate markets.

1. Affordable Housing

As cities grow, the demand for affordable housing often outpaces supply. Governments implement policies like rent controls and inclusionary zoning (Chapter 6) to address this issue, but these measures can also impact market dynamics.

2. Traffic Congestion

Urbanization increases traffic congestion, reducing quality of life and property values in affected areas. Investments in public transportation and road networks are critical to mitigating this issue.

3. Environmental Concerns

Urban development can strain natural resources and contribute to pollution. Incorporating green building practices and sustainable planning is essential for long-term urban growth.

Case Studies: Urban Economics in Action

1. London's Crossrail Project

The Crossrail project, a new railway network in London, demonstrates the impact of infrastructure on real estate markets.

Properties near Crossrail stations experienced significant value appreciation, highlighting the importance of connectivity in urban development.

2. The Transformation of Detroit

Detroit's urban renewal initiatives, including investments in downtown redevelopment and affordable housing, illustrate the potential for revitalizing struggling cities.

These efforts have attracted new residents and businesses, reshaping the city's real estate market.

The Role of Valuation in Urban Development

Real estate valuation, discussed in Chapter 7, is a cornerstone of urban economics.

Accurate valuations inform decisions about land use, infrastructure investment, and project feasibility.

- For Developers: Valuations guide site selection and project planning.
- For Governments: Valuations support tax assessments and resource allocation.
- For Investors: Valuations provide insights into market potential and risk.

As we transition to Chapter 9, the role of valuation becomes even more complex in global markets, where urbanization trends vary across regions.

Practical Applications: Navigating Urban Economics

Understanding urban economics and development principles can help you identify opportunities and mitigate risks in real estate markets.

- For Buyers: Look for neighborhoods benefiting from infrastructure investments or urban renewal initiatives.
- For Investors: Focus on areas with strong economic clusters and population growth.
- For Developers: Align projects with urban planning goals to secure permits and attract buyers or tenants.

Conclusion: Cities as Engines of Growth

Urban economics is the study of how cities grow, function, and evolve, and real estate is at the heart of this dynamic process.

From infrastructure investments to zoning regulations, urban planning shapes the opportunities and challenges in real estate markets.

As we move into the next chapter, we'll expand our perspective to explore global real estate markets.

You'll discover how urbanization trends, cultural preferences, and economic conditions vary across regions, creating unique dynamics and opportunities.

Keep reading, because understanding urban economics is just the beginning. The global stage awaits, and with it, new insights into the ever-changing world of real estate.

Chapter 9: Global Real Estate Markets

Real estate is inherently local, rooted in the unique characteristics of individual cities, neighborhoods, and even streets.

Yet, in today's interconnected world, real estate markets are no longer confined by geography. They are influenced by global trends, cross-border investments, and economic dynamics that transcend national boundaries.

For those who venture into the world of international real estate, opportunities abound, along with unique challenges. Understanding the global real estate landscape is crucial for identifying investment prospects, mitigating risks, and navigating the complexities of cross-border transactions.

This chapter explores the dynamics of global real estate markets, offering insights into how they operate, what drives them, and how to approach them strategically.

What Makes International Real Estate Unique?

Global real estate markets differ from local markets in several key ways, driven by diverse factors such as cultural preferences, economic policies, and geopolitical conditions.

While the fundamentals of supply, demand, and valuation apply universally, the context varies significantly across regions.

1. Diverse Market Dynamics

Each country has its own real estate regulations, tax systems, and market drivers. For example:

- Emerging Markets: Countries like India, Brazil, and Vietnam offer high-growth opportunities due to rapid urbanization and population expansion.
- Developed Markets: Established markets like the United States, Germany, and Japan provide stability and mature infrastructure but may have slower growth.

2. Currency Fluctuations

Currency exchange rates play a critical role in international real estate investments.

A strong domestic currency can make foreign properties more affordable, while a weak currency may increase costs. Investors must account for these fluctuations when assessing returns.

3. Cultural Preferences

Cultural differences influence real estate preferences.

For instance, in some Asian markets, buyers place a premium on properties with auspicious numbers or specific layouts, while in Western markets, functionality and location may carry greater weight.

Drivers of Global Real Estate Markets

Understanding the forces that shape global real estate markets is essential for identifying opportunities and risks.

1. Economic Growth and Urbanization

Rapid economic growth and urbanization are driving real estate development in many emerging markets. Cities like Shanghai, Lagos, and São Paulo are experiencing unprecedented demand for housing, offices, and retail spaces, fueled by expanding middle classes and increased consumer spending.

2. Cross-Border Investments

Cross-border investments have surged in recent decades, with institutional investors, high-net-worth individuals, and real estate funds seeking diversification and higher returns. For example, Chinese investors have been major players in global markets, acquiring properties in cities like London, New York, and Sydney.

3. Technology and Connectivity

Technology is breaking down barriers to international real estate investment. Online platforms and digital tools make it easier to research, transact, and manage properties across borders. Blockchain technology is also emerging as a solution for secure and transparent international transactions.

4. Geopolitical Factors

Geopolitical events, such as trade agreements, sanctions, and political instability, can significantly impact global real estate markets. For instance, Brexit created uncertainty in the UK property market, while trade tensions between the US and China influenced cross-border investments.

Asset-Backed Mortgages in International Markets

Asset-backed mortgages (ABMs) are a significant feature of global real estate markets, offering unique financing opportunities and challenges.

What Are Asset-Backed Mortgages?

Asset-backed mortgages are loans secured by real estate assets.

Unlike traditional mortgages, which may rely primarily on income verification, ABMs use the value of the property as collateral.

This makes them an attractive option for international investors, who may face difficulties meeting local income requirements.

Benefits of Asset-Backed Mortgages

1. Flexibility for Investors: ABMs provide financing options for non-residents and foreign nationals investing in overseas markets.
2. Reduced Risk for Lenders: By securing loans against high-value properties, lenders mitigate the risk of default.

3. Access to Global Opportunities: Investors can leverage ABMs to expand their portfolios across borders.

Challenges of Asset-Backed Mortgages

- Regulatory Differences: ABM structures vary by country, requiring investors to navigate complex legal frameworks.
- Currency Risks: Loan repayments in foreign currencies can expose borrowers to exchange rate fluctuations.
- Higher Interest Rates: Lenders may charge premium rates for ABMs, reflecting the perceived risk of cross-border lending.

ABMs are an essential tool for international investors, but they require careful consideration of local regulations and market conditions.

Strategies for Navigating Global Real Estate Markets

Successfully navigating global real estate markets requires a combination of market knowledge, strategic planning, and risk management.

1. Research Local Markets

Understanding local market dynamics is crucial. Consider factors like:

- Property demand and supply.
- Regulatory frameworks and tax policies.
- Cultural preferences and economic trends.

2. Diversify Investments

Diversification reduces risk by spreading investments across multiple markets. For example, combining high-growth properties in emerging markets with stable assets in developed countries creates a balanced portfolio.

3. Leverage Professional Networks

Working with local real estate agents, legal advisors, and property managers can provide valuable insights and streamline the investment process.

4. Monitor Global Trends

Staying informed about global economic and geopolitical developments helps anticipate market shifts and identify opportunities.

Case Studies: Global Real Estate Dynamics

1. Dubai's Property Market

Dubai's real estate market exemplifies the impact of international investment and government policies. Tax incentives, visa reforms, and strategic location have attracted investors from around the world, creating a dynamic and competitive market.

2. Tokyo's Housing Stability

Despite Japan's aging population and declining birthrate, Tokyo's property market remains stable, driven by strong demand for urban housing and government policies promoting redevelopment.

Practical Applications: Leveraging Global Markets

For Investors

- Identify markets with high growth potential or undervalued properties.
- Use asset-backed mortgages to finance international acquisitions.

For Developers

- Align projects with local market demands and cultural preferences.
- Leverage global trends, such as sustainable development and smart cities.

For Buyers

- Evaluate currency risks and financing options.
- Research local tax implications and regulatory requirements.

Conclusion: The World at Your Doorstep

The global real estate market offers unparalleled opportunities for growth, diversification, and innovation.

By understanding the unique dynamics of international markets and leveraging tools like asset-backed mortgages, you can unlock the potential of cross-border investments.

As we move into the final chapters of this book, we'll shift our focus to future trends in real estate economics, exploring how technology, sustainability, and shifting demographics will reshape markets worldwide.

These insights will build on the foundation of global dynamics, providing a roadmap for navigating the challenges and opportunities ahead.

The journey through real estate economics is far from over. Keep reading to discover what lies on the horizon and how you can prepare for the next evolution in this dynamic industry.

Chapter 10: The Drivers of Future Trends in Real Estate

The future of real estate economics will be shaped by a combination of technological innovation, demographic shifts, and global economic forces. These drivers are already influencing markets worldwide, and their impact will only grow in the coming decades.

1. Technology and Innovation

Technology has already revolutionized how real estate is bought, sold, and managed, and its influence will only deepen. As we explored in Chapter 9, advancements like blockchain and online platforms are making international transactions more accessible. Looking forward, technologies such as artificial intelligence (AI), virtual reality (VR), and the Internet of Things (IoT) will play an even greater role.

- AI and Big Data: Predictive analytics will allow investors and developers to forecast market trends with greater accuracy, identifying

opportunities before they become mainstream.
- Virtual Reality: VR will transform property marketing, enabling buyers to explore properties remotely through immersive virtual tours.
- Smart Buildings: IoT devices will make buildings more efficient, reducing energy consumption and enhancing tenant experiences.

2. Sustainability and Green Development

Sustainability is no longer a trend, it's a necessity. Governments and consumers alike are demanding greener, more energy-efficient properties, as discussed in Chapter 8 on urban economics.

- Net-Zero Buildings: Future developments will increasingly focus on achieving net-zero carbon emissions, leveraging renewable energy and sustainable materials.
- Eco-Cities: Urban planners are designing entire neighborhoods with sustainability in mind, integrating green spaces, efficient transport systems, and renewable energy sources.

These trends will reshape urban landscapes and influence valuation methods, as properties that meet sustainability criteria are likely to command higher prices.

3. Demographic Shifts

Demographics play a critical role in shaping real estate markets, and future changes will have profound implications.

- Aging Populations: In many developed countries, aging populations will drive demand for senior housing, healthcare facilities, and age-friendly urban designs.
- Millennial and Gen Z Buyers: Younger generations prioritize flexibility and technology, influencing demand for co-living spaces, remote work setups, and smart homes.
- Urbanization in Emerging Markets: Rapid urbanization in countries like India and Nigeria will create opportunities for large-scale housing developments and infrastructure projects.

4. Globalization and Cross-Border Investments

As discussed in Chapter 9, global real estate markets are becoming increasingly interconnected. In the future, this trend will accelerate, driven by advancements in technology and shifts in economic power.

- Global Investment Hubs: Cities like Singapore, Dubai, and London will continue to attract cross-border investments, while new hubs emerge in developing markets.
- Geopolitical Factors: Trade agreements, sanctions, and political shifts will shape the flow of international capital into real estate.

Emerging Trends in Real Estate Development

1. Mixed-Use Developments

Mixed-use developments, which combine residential, commercial, and recreational spaces, are gaining popularity. These projects cater to the growing demand for convenience and walkability, especially in urban areas.

2. Smart Cities

Smart cities integrate technology into urban infrastructure to improve efficiency, sustainability, and quality of life. As discussed in Chapter 8, smart city initiatives will drive demand for innovative real estate solutions, from energy-efficient buildings to intelligent transport systems.

3. Affordable Housing Innovations

Addressing the global housing crisis will require innovative solutions, such as modular construction, 3D printing, and public-private partnerships. These approaches will reduce construction costs and accelerate project timelines.

4. Remote Work and Suburbanization

The shift toward remote work, accelerated by the COVID-19 pandemic, is reshaping real estate demand. Suburban and rural areas are experiencing a resurgence as people seek larger homes and quieter environments. T

his trend, explored in earlier chapters, will continue to influence market cycles and valuation strategies.

Predictions for Future Real Estate Markets

1. Increased Digitalization

Digital tools and platforms will dominate real estate transactions, from blockchain-based property registries to AI-driven market analysis. These technologies will increase transparency, reduce transaction costs, and improve efficiency.

2. Greater Focus on Wellness

Post-pandemic, wellness-oriented properties will become a priority. Developments will emphasize natural light, green spaces, and wellness amenities to meet consumer demand for healthier living environments.

3. Decentralized Urbanization

While urban centers will remain vital, decentralized urbanization will gain traction. Smaller cities and towns, supported by infrastructure improvements, will attract populations from congested megacities.

Asset-Backed Mortgages and Future Financing Innovations

Building on the discussion of asset-backed mortgages (Chapter 9), future financing solutions will become more flexible and globally accessible.

- Blockchain for Mortgages: Blockchain technology will streamline loan processes, reducing paperwork and improving security.
- Fractional Ownership Models: Investors will be able to purchase fractional shares of properties, democratizing access to high-value real estate.
- Green Financing: Lenders will increasingly offer incentives for sustainable developments, aligning financing with environmental goals.

Opportunities in Future Real Estate Markets

Understanding future trends is not just about prediction, it's about identifying opportunities.

- For Investors: Diversify portfolios by targeting emerging markets, sustainable developments, and technology-driven projects.
- For Developers: Embrace innovations in construction and design to stay competitive in a rapidly changing landscape.
- For Policymakers: Collaborate with private sectors to address housing shortages, improve infrastructure, and promote sustainability.

Practical Case Studies

1. The Rise of Vertical Cities

Cities like Singapore and Tokyo are embracing vertical urbanization, creating high-density developments with integrated amenities.

These projects maximize land use and reflect the principles of urban economics discussed earlier.

2. Africa's Urban Boom

Emerging markets in Africa are experiencing rapid urbanization, driving demand for affordable housing, commercial spaces, and infrastructure.

Investors and developers who enter these markets early stand to gain significant returns.

Conclusion: The Road Ahead

The future of real estate economics is a story of innovation, adaptation, and growth.

From sustainability and smart cities to demographic shifts and global investments, the trends shaping the industry are as diverse as the markets they influence.

As we near the end of this book, the insights from this chapter connect back to everything we've explored, from valuation methods and urban planning to global market dynamics.

The tools and knowledge you've gained will prepare you to navigate the challenges and opportunities that lie ahead.

But the journey isn't over yet. In the final chapters, we'll consolidate these lessons, offering strategies for applying them in real-world scenarios.

Keep reading, because the best way to predict the future of real estate is to understand the forces shaping it today.

Chapter 11: Final Thoughts and Summary

Real estate economics is a field as dynamic as the markets it seeks to understand.

Over the course of this book, we've delved into the intricate forces that shape real estate, from fundamental principles like supply and demand to global trends and emerging innovations.

This chapter serves as both a summary and a reflection, tying together the key insights we've explored while providing a roadmap for how to apply them in the real estate world.

Whether you are a homeowner, investor, developer, or simply someone with an interest in real estate, understanding these principles is more than academic.

It's about equipping yourself with the tools to navigate a constantly evolving industry with confidence and foresight.

Key Lessons from the Journey

As we reflect on the journey through this book, several recurring themes emerge, each reinforcing the complexity and interconnectedness of real estate economics.

1. Understanding Market Dynamics

At the heart of real estate economics lies the balance of supply and demand.

Markets are shaped by these forces, influenced by factors as varied as population growth, income levels, and government policies.

By grasping the dynamics of supply and demand, you can better anticipate price trends and identify investment opportunities.

Yet, these dynamics do not exist in isolation. They are affected by broader economic indicators, such as interest rates, employment levels, and GDP growth.

Understanding how these indicators influence real estate markets provides a framework for making informed decisions, whether buying, selling, or investing.

2. The Power of Location

Location is a cornerstone of real estate valuation and desirability. As we've seen, proximity to amenities, infrastructure, and economic hubs drives demand, shaping property values over time.

Urban planning and infrastructure investments play a critical role here, transforming neighborhoods and creating opportunities for growth.

This interplay between location and value underscores the importance of staying informed about urban development projects and planning initiatives.

By keeping an eye on these factors, you can position yourself to capitalize on emerging trends in your local market.

3. Valuation as a Strategic Tool

Accurately valuing real estate is essential for making sound decisions. Valuation methods, whether based on comparable sales, income potential, or replacement costs, provide a foundation for understanding a property's worth.

These tools are not just for appraisers; they are vital for anyone navigating the real estate market.

Valuation also connects to the broader trends shaping real estate economics. For instance, sustainability and smart cities are redefining what makes a property valuable.

As global markets evolve, valuation methods must adapt to account for these changes.

4. Navigating Global Real Estate Markets

Real estate is no longer confined to local markets. Globalization has made it possible to invest in properties across borders, but this comes with unique challenges.

Currency fluctuations, cultural differences, and varying regulatory environments require careful navigation.

At the same time, international markets offer opportunities for diversification and growth.

Emerging markets, in particular, present exciting prospects for investors willing to take calculated risks.

Understanding global market dynamics is key to unlocking these opportunities.

5. The Role of Innovation

Technology is reshaping real estate in profound ways, from virtual reality tours to blockchain-enabled transactions. These innovations are making markets more transparent, efficient, and accessible.

Looking ahead, the integration of artificial intelligence, the Internet of Things, and sustainable building practices will continue to drive change.

Staying abreast of these advancements is critical for staying competitive in the real estate industry.

Six Practical Next Steps for Moving Forward

With the insights gained from this book, you are now better equipped to navigate the complexities of real estate economics. Here are some practical steps to apply these principles in the real world:

1. Stay Informed

Real estate markets are constantly changing. Keep up with economic indicators, government policies, and market trends to stay ahead of the curve. Regularly review industry reports, news articles, and market analyses to refine your understanding.

2. Analyze Opportunities

When considering a property, evaluate its potential through multiple lenses, location, valuation, and market dynamics. Use tools like comparable sales and income projections to assess its value and future potential.

3. Think Long-Term

Real estate is a long-term investment. Focus on properties and markets with strong fundamentals, and avoid being swayed by short-term fluctuations or speculative trends. Consider how factors like urbanization, infrastructure development, and sustainability will impact value over time.

4. Diversify Your Portfolio

If you're an investor, diversification is key to managing risk. Look beyond local markets to explore opportunities in emerging and global markets, balancing high-growth prospects with stable assets.

5. Leverage Professional Networks

Real estate is a collaborative industry. Build relationships with local agents, appraisers, and legal professionals to gain insights and access to opportunities. In global markets, partner with experts who understand the nuances of local regulations and cultural preferences.

6. Embrace Technology

Leverage digital tools to streamline your real estate transactions and management. Whether it's using virtual tours to explore properties or blockchain for secure transactions, embracing technology will keep you ahead in an increasingly digital market.

The Future of Real Estate Economics

While this book has provided a comprehensive overview of real estate economics, the journey doesn't end here.

The industry will continue to evolve, shaped by trends such as sustainability, smart cities, and demographic shifts. By staying adaptable and informed, you can thrive in this ever-changing landscape.

As you look to the future, consider the role of education and collaboration.

Whether you're attending industry conferences, participating in webinars, or engaging with peers, continuous learning is essential for staying relevant in real estate.

Conclusion: Building Your Real Estate Roadmap

Real estate economics is more than a study of markets; it's a blueprint for understanding how people, policies, and places intersect to shape the built environment.

The insights you've gained from this book are tools to navigate this complex world, whether you're a first-time buyer, a seasoned investor, or someone exploring opportunities across borders.

As you turn the pages, remember that this is not the end of your journey, it's the beginning of a new phase in your understanding of real estate.

Armed with knowledge and perspective, you are now prepared to identify opportunities, mitigate risks, and contribute to the ever-evolving world of real estate economics.

Keep learning, keep exploring, and keep building your roadmap for success.

Chapter 12: Conclusion and Call to Action

As I completed Chapter 11, reflecting on the journey we've taken through this book, it struck me that a small call to action was already present in the summary.

But I felt it deserved more attention, more space to breathe. After all, a book like this isn't just about understanding the concepts of real estate economics, it's about applying them.

It's about translating knowledge into action, about shaping your own path in the dynamic, ever-changing world of real estate.

First, let me say thank you. If you've made it this far, it means you've not only read the book but engaged with its ideas.

You've navigated supply and demand dynamics, explored global markets, and considered the impact of technology and sustainability on real estate. It's no small feat to take on a subject as intricate and multifaceted as real estate economics, and I'm truly grateful for your time and curiosity.

Now, as we close this journey, I invite you to take the lessons you've learned and apply them in the real world. Whether you're an investor, developer, or simply someone with a keen interest in real estate, the knowledge you've gained is your foundation.

The journey through these pages was designed to provide a roadmap, but now it's time to create your own.

Begin by reflecting on the insights that resonated most with you. Was it the analysis of market cycles and trends? Or perhaps the role of valuation in shaping investment decisions?

Whatever stood out, start there. Deepen your understanding by researching your local market or exploring opportunities in areas of interest. This process doesn't end with reading; it begins with action.

For those considering investments, revisit the sections on valuation and market dynamics. Assess properties not just for their present value but for their long-term potential.

Consider how sustainability, urban development, or global trends might enhance or challenge their worth over time. If you're already a property owner, think about how urban planning or infrastructure changes in your area could affect your investment.

If you're new to real estate, start small but think big. Explore local markets, familiarize yourself with the role of economic indicators, and take the first steps toward understanding the forces at play. This book has laid the groundwork, but the next step is yours to take.

For readers with a keen interest in global markets, I encourage you to explore the nuances of cross-border investments and the cultural differences that shape real estate preferences. The chapter on global real estate markets was just the beginning.

There is a world of opportunity waiting, and your next move might be as simple as attending a seminar, connecting with an international agent, or investigating asset-backed mortgages in a foreign country.

And for those fascinated by the future of real estate, now is the time to embrace innovation. Dive deeper into technology trends, consider how AI or blockchain could influence your strategy, and look for opportunities in sustainable developments or smart cities.

The future of real estate economics is being written every day, and you have the chance to be part of that story.

Throughout this book, I've emphasized the importance of staying informed, of being adaptable, and of continuously learning. The world of real estate is not static. It evolves with economies, technologies, and societies. Keep your eyes open, your mind curious, and your skills sharp.

Finally, I hope this isn't the last real estate book you will read. *Real Estate Economics* is just one piece of a much larger puzzle, and I encourage you to explore the rest of my real estate books and other resources that complement what you've learned here.

Whether you're looking for a deeper dive into valuation methods, a closer examination of urban development, or a broader exploration of strategies for navigating market cycles and investment opportunities, there is always more to discover.

Let this be the beginning of an ongoing journey into understanding and mastering the fascinating world of real estate.

So, thank you once again for taking this journey with me. The next steps are yours to take, but I'll leave you with this thought: Real estate is more than transactions and trends. It's about building something lasting, something meaningful, whether that's a portfolio, a community, or simply your understanding of the world.

Let this book be your starting point, and let the glossary that follows be your quick reference as you embark on what comes next.

And who knows? Maybe we'll meet again in another book, another chapter, or another journey into the fascinating world of real estate.

Glossary of Key Words

The world of real estate economics is built on precise language. Each term carries weight, shaping how professionals, investors, and policymakers interpret markets and make decisions.

This glossary is designed to clarify the key concepts, technical terms, and financial principles used throughout the book.

Whether you are a student, practitioner, or curious reader, these definitions will help you understand the terminology behind property valuation, investment strategy, and market dynamics, allowing you to read, analyze, and apply real estate economics with confidence.

Absorption Rate: The speed at which available properties are sold or leased within a specific market and time period. It indicates the balance between supply and demand.

Amortization: The gradual repayment of a loan's principal and interest through regular installments, most often associated with mortgages.

Arbitrage in Real Estate: Exploiting price differences between similar assets or markets to achieve profit without proportional risk.

Asset-Backed Securities (ABS): Financial instruments secured by income-producing real estate assets, such as mortgages or leases.

Building Efficiency Ratio (BER): The proportion of a building's net usable area to its gross floor area, reflecting how efficiently space is utilized.

Capital Expenditure (CapEx): Funds used to acquire, upgrade, or maintain physical assets such as buildings or infrastructure.

Capitalization Rate (Cap Rate): A measure used to estimate investment returns, calculated as net operating income divided by current property value.

Comparable Sales (Comps): The analysis of similar properties recently sold to determine the fair market value of a subject property.

Construction Inflation: The increase in material, labor, and compliance costs that affects overall project viability and profitability.

Core, Core-Plus, Value-Add, Opportunistic Investments: Classifications describing different real estate investment risk and return profiles, ranging from stable income-producing assets to high-risk redevelopment projects.

Demand Elasticity: The responsiveness of property demand to changes in price, income, or other economic variables.

Economic Base Theory: The principle that local economic growth depends on basic industries that attract external income and stimulate non-basic local services.

Economic Rent: Income earned from the ownership of land or property due to its scarcity, desirability, or location advantage.

Effective Gross Income (EGI): The total income a property generates, including rent and ancillary revenues, minus vacancy and collection losses.

Fiscal Policy: Government use of spending and taxation to influence economic activity, indirectly shaping real estate markets.

Gross Leasable Area (GLA): The total floor space designed for tenant occupancy and exclusive use, typically measured in square meters or feet.

Highest and Best Use (HBU): The most profitable, legally permissible, and physically possible use of a property.

Hedonic Pricing Model: A valuation method that isolates the contribution of specific features (location, amenities, size) to a property's price.

Land Banking: The strategic acquisition and holding of undeveloped land for future development or sale.

Land Use Economics: The study of how land resources are allocated among competing uses such as residential, commercial, and industrial.

Leverage: Using borrowed funds to increase the potential return on investment in property acquisitions or developments.

Liquidity in Real Estate: The ease with which a property can be sold or refinanced without significantly affecting its market price.

Market Absorption: The rate at which new or existing space in a market is leased or sold during a specific time frame.

Market Equilibrium: The condition in which property supply and demand are balanced, resulting in price stability.

Monetary Policy: Central bank actions, such as adjusting interest rates, that influence credit availability and real estate activity.

Net Operating Income (NOI): Total income generated by a property after deducting operating expenses but before financing costs and taxes.

Opportunity Cost of Land: The value of the next-best alternative use forgone when land is developed for a specific purpose.

Real Estate Cycle: The recurring stages of expansion, peak, contraction, and recovery that characterize property markets.

Real Estate Investment Trust (REIT): A company that owns, operates, or finances income-producing properties and distributes profits to investors.

Risk Premium: The extra return investors expect to compensate for the risk of real estate investment compared with risk-free assets.

Spatial Economics: The study of how geographic factors and location decisions affect land use and property values.

Speculative Development: Construction undertaken without pre-leased tenants or secured buyers, based on anticipated future demand.

Systemic Risk: The risk that instability in real estate markets could trigger broader financial system disruptions.

Vacancy Rate: The percentage of all available rental units in a market that are unoccupied at a given time.

Yield on Cost (YoC): A measure comparing a development's net operating income to its total project cost, used to evaluate feasibility.

Zoning: Local government regulation that dictates how specific parcels of land can be used, such as for residential, commercial, or industrial purposes.

Additional Advanced Terms

Depreciation: The gradual decrease in a property's value due to physical wear, functional obsolescence, or external factors.

Discounted Cash Flow (DCF): A financial model that determines the present value of future cash flows generated by a real estate investment.

Feasibility Study: A comprehensive analysis that assesses the practicality and profitability of a proposed real estate development.

Gross Development Value (GDV): The total estimated value of a completed property development, used to evaluate project viability.

Internal Rate of Return (IRR): The discount rate that makes the net present value (NPV) of all future cash flows from an investment equal to zero.

Loan-to-Value Ratio (LTV): A financial metric expressing the ratio of a loan amount to the appraised value of the property securing the loan.

Replacement Cost: The estimated cost to rebuild a property of similar utility using current construction methods and materials.

Return on Investment (ROI): The percentage gain or loss on an investment relative to its cost, used to measure performance efficiency.

Tenure System: The legal framework defining ownership and occupancy rights, such as freehold, leasehold, or sectional title.

Vacancy Absorption Ratio: The relationship between newly occupied space and the amount of vacant space available, indicating the pace of market recovery.

Acknowledgements

Writing *Real Estate Economics* has been a profound journey, not only in articulating the principles and complexities of this fascinating field but also in reflecting on the extraordinary individuals who have shaped my understanding and perspective. This book would not have been possible without the wisdom, guidance, and collaboration of the brilliant minds who have crossed my path, economists, financial directors, urban planners, policymakers, and business leaders from across the globe.

To the economists whose insights have deepened my understanding of market dynamics and global trends, thank you for your contributions to the foundational concepts woven throughout this book. Your ability to interpret the intricate dance of supply, demand, and valuation has been a source of inspiration. To the financial directors and industry leaders with whom I've had the privilege of working, your expertise in navigating global markets and strategic investments has profoundly influenced the sections on international real estate and asset-backed mortgages.

To urban planners and policymakers, whose vision and commitment to sustainable development have redefined the cities of tomorrow, I owe a debt of gratitude. Your work has illuminated the chapters on urban economics and infrastructure, underscoring how thoughtful planning can shape vibrant and equitable communities.

I also want to extend my heartfelt thanks to the international companies and institutions that have invited me into their boardrooms, their projects, and their strategies. From global developers driving innovation to the political leaders championing housing and economic reforms, your efforts have enriched this book and made its scope truly global.

Of course, I must acknowledge the countless colleagues, peers, and mentors who have shared their time, expertise, and support. Some of these chapters, particularly those on valuation methods, government regulations, and future trends, are enriched by your direct contributions and insights. You know who you are, and I am sincerely grateful for your role in this endeavor.

Lastly, to every reader, whether you are a student of real estate, a seasoned professional, or someone exploring this field for the first time, thank you for your curiosity and engagement. This book was written with you in mind, and it is my hope that the knowledge within these pages empowers you to navigate real estate economics with confidence and clarity.

To all who have played a role in this work, directly or indirectly, I extend my deepest appreciation. This book is as much a reflection of your brilliance as it is of my own journey through this complex and captivating industry. Thank you.

Willem Tait

Social Profiles

Willem Tait is committed to staying connected and engaging with his readers. He is active on LinkedIn and X (formerly Twitter), where he shares updates on his latest projects, insights, and resources. Willem is also available for face-to-face consultations, public speaking, and group training sessions through platforms like WhatsApp, Zoom, Google Meet, and Microsoft Teams.

Feel free to reach out on any of these platforms to connect, share ideas, or discuss opportunities for learning and growth. Let's keep building together!

Linktree: https://linktr.ee/willemtait
Linkedin: https://www.linkedin.com/in/willemtait
X: https://x.com/willemtait
Amazon Author: https://www.amazon.com/author/willemtait
Goodreads Author: https://www.goodreads.com/willemtait
Calendly https://calendly.com/willemtait
Blogger: https://willemtaitauthor.blogspot.com/
Substack: https://willemtait.substack.com/
Medium: https://willemtaitblog.medium.com/
Pinterest: https://.pinterest.com/willemtait/

Mentorship, Coaching, Consulting and Public Speaking

As a dedicated professional with a passion for real estate, business, law, and economics, I thrive on sharing actionable insights and practical strategies that empower individuals and teams to achieve their goals.

My expertise spans real estate investment, business consulting, personal growth, and the intricate connections between legal and economic frameworks, allowing me to offer a well-rounded perspective tailored to diverse challenges and ambitions.

Through public speaking engagements, customised mentorship programs, and dynamic one-on-one or group coaching sessions, I aim to inspire, educate, and guide. Whether addressing an audience of hundreds or working closely with a small team, my mission is to deliver value-driven insights that leave a lasting impact.

If you're seeking a keynote speaker to energise and inform your event, a consultant to elevate your business strategies, or a mentor to foster personal and professional growth, I'm here to collaborate. My approach integrates years of hands-on experience with a solid foundation in real estate, law and economics, ensuring the strategies I share are both practical and informed by robust principles.

Let's connect to explore how I can help you or your organisation unlock new opportunities and achieve meaningful success. Together, we can create strategies that inspire growth, drive innovation, and deliver measurable results.

LinkedIn: https://www.linkedin.com/in/willemtait/

Mail: willemtait@outlook.com

About the Author

Willem Tait is an accomplished author, real estate expert, and industry mentor whose journey through the worlds of property investment, real estate development, capital markets, and human understanding has inspired professionals across the globe. With decades of experience, Willem has become a trusted voice in real estate strategy, capital markets integration, and the transformative power of mentorship, all underpinned by a deep interest in psychology, philosophy, and the profound connections between people and spaces.

Willem's passion for education, critical thinking, and professional growth is reflected in the nine insightful books authored to date. Each work delves into the intricate dynamics of real estate while exploring the psychological and philosophical forces that shape decision-making and human interaction. Offering practical strategies, actionable insights, and thought-provoking perspectives, Willem's writings span topics from sustainability and innovation to navigating complex financial landscapes. This prolific body of work solidifies his position as an authority in the field, bridging the gap between theory, practice, and the human experience with clarity and expertise.

Beyond writing, Willem Tait holds a strong academic foundation, having pursued advanced studies that inform a nuanced understanding of real estate, economics, psychology, and philosophy. This dedication to lifelong learning complements a hands-on approach to mentoring aspiring professionals, helping them achieve their goals in real estate and beyond. Known for his ability to break down complex concepts into accessible knowledge, Willem empowers readers and mentees alike to navigate the evolving challenges of the industry while fostering a deeper understanding of the motivations and principles that drive success.

Whether guiding readers through the intricacies of capital markets, exploring the philosophical meaning of spaces, or inspiring the next generation of leaders, Willem Tait continues to shape the conversation around real estate and its future. This blend of expertise, passion, and a commitment to human connection ensures that Willem remains not just a specialist, but a trailblazer in the ever-changing world of real estate, capital markets, and the broader human narrative.

List of Books to Date

Willem Tait is the author of several impactful real estate books that examine the dynamic and ever-changing nature of the real estate market. Each book provides valuable strategies, practical insights, and a comprehensive understanding of the key factors influencing the industry. Below is the full list of his published works to date:

Real Estate Law Essentials:
Navigate Cross-Sections, Avoid Pitfalls, and Seize Opportunities. A comprehensive guide to understanding the legal frameworks surrounding real estate, offering practical advice for navigating transactions and mitigating risks.

Proven Principles of Residential Real Estate Investment:
Strategies and Tasks for Building Generational Wealth. A detailed exploration of residential real estate investment strategies, designed to help readers achieve long-term financial security and success.

Practical Principles of Commercial Real Estate Investment:
Tasks and Strategies for Real Estate Success. Focused on commercial real estate, this book provides actionable principles and strategies for navigating the complexities of the market and achieving professional growth.

Real Estate Economics:
Property Market Principles and Practices. This book offers an informative, in-depth analysis of real estate markets, their practices and their underlying principles, and the economic forces driving them.

Raising Money for Real Estate Investment:
Close Deals, Raise Money, Build Wealth. A practical guide to securing funding for real estate projects, this book emphasizes effective deal-making and wealth-building strategies.

Capital Markets and Real Estate:
Bridging Markets for a Global Future. This work explores the intersection of real estate and capital markets, highlighting their convergence and the opportunities that globalization presents for industry professionals.

Real Estate Development and Deal Making:
The Essential Guide for Property Developers, Entrepreneurs, and Dealmakers. This comprehensive guide ties together the foundational principles of property development with innovative strategies for deal-making and entrepreneurship, providing actionable insights for success in the industry.

Psychology of Residential and Commercial Real Estate:
Master the Psychology Behind Real Estate Success. A practical guide into real estate decision making. By uncovering the emotions, motivations, and cognitive biases behind property decisions, this book provides actionable strategies for property success.

Philosophy of Residential and Commercial Real Estate:
Exploring the Intersection of Philosophy, People, Property, Purpose and Spaces. A thoughtful exploration of the deeper meaning behind property and spaces. By examining the beliefs, values, and purposes that shape real estate, this book provides insightful principles for aligning property decisions with vision and intent.

Economics of Banking and Money:
Explores how money and banking shape modern economies. From currency's origins to digital finance, it demystifies complex topics and connects them to daily life. An essential guide for students and curious readers, it shows how trust and innovation drive finance.

Real Estate Mastery Books Series

These books are part of the Real Estate Mastery Books, a series designed to equip readers with the tools and knowledge necessary to excel in the fields of real estate and capital markets. This ever-expanding series reflects Willem Tait's commitment to providing actionable insights and strategies. Keep an eye out for upcoming titles in this growing collection, as there are always more exciting additions to come.

We Value your Feedback

Thank you for taking the time to read *Real Estate Economics*. Your thoughts and reflections mean a great deal to me. If you found the ideas and insights in this book helpful, please consider leaving a review or rating on Amazon or Goodreads.

Your feedback not only helps other readers discover valuable resources but also guides me in shaping future books that better serve you and the real estate community.

Amazon Author:
https://www.amazon.com/author/willemtait

Goodreads Author:
https://www.goodreads.com/willemtait

Portfolio of Books by Willem Tait

For more, kindly see www.amazon.com/author/willemtait

BUSINESS BOOKS

1. **Real Estate Law Essentials:** Navigate Cross-Sections, Avoid Pitfalls, and Seize Opportunities.
2. **Proven Principles of Residential Real Estate Investment:** Strategies and Tasks for Building Generational Wealth.
3. **Practical Principles of Commercial Real Estate Investment:** Tasks and Strategies for Real Estate Success.
4. **Real Estate Economics:** Property Market Principles and Practices.
5. **Raising Money for Real Estate Investment:** Close Deals, Raise Money, Build Wealth.
6. **Capital Markets and Real Estate:** How Money and Capital Shapes the Property Market.
7. **Real Estate Development and Deal Making:** The Essential Guide for Property Developers, Entrepreneurs, and Dealmakers.
8. **Psychology of Residential and Commercial Real Estate:** Master the Psychology Behind Real Estate Success.
9. **Philosophy of Residential and Commercial Real Estate:** Exploring the Intersection of Philosophy, People, Property, Purpose and Spaces.
10. **Economics of Banking and Money:** Insight into Power, Trust, and Change.
11. **The Future of Real Estate:** PropTech, Sustainability and Design

SELF-HELP AND MOTIVATIONAL BOOKS

1. **Sort Your Crap Out:** Own Your Choices, Silence Your Critic. Get Stuff Done
2. **Dammit, Get It Together:** Stop Making Excuses and Start Living the Life You Deserve
3. **Stop Giving a Damn and Start Living:** Cut thffe Crap. Focus on What Matters. Live Fully
4. **Dammit, It's Your Life:** Own Your Mind, Time, and Choices
5. **Dammit, Stop Being Overwhelmed and Overworked:** Reclaim Your Time, Energy, and Sanity

ANNOTATED AND COMMENTARY

1. **The Way to Wealth** (Annotated): With Motivational Commentary by Willem Tait
2. **The Art Of War:** (Annotated): Proven Modern Strategies for Winning in Business, Leadership, and Life by Willem Tait

www.ingramcontent.com/pod-product-compliance
Lightning Source LLC
Chambersburg PA
CBHW052256220526
45471CB00001B/362